Table of Contents

Introduction

I want to thank you and congratulate you for downloading the book, *"CANNABIS: The Beginners Guide on How to Start Growing Marijuana Plants at Home"*.

This book contains easy steps on how to start growing marijuana plants at home and everything you need to know about the plant and its needs.

It offers an step by step guide divided in the 4 main stages of growing a plant which are: Preparation, Germination, Vegetation and The harvest. Including all the materials that you will need, the most common mistakes to avoid when growing marijuana and a lot of useful tips. Also, all along this book you will found a lot of images that will help you understand the explanations and procedures.

In this guide you will find ways of growing a plant that gives excellent results. Those who cultivated the plant know that there is a bunch of data on the cultivation and you can be confused, so you have to pick your way and smart tips that are always welcome!

Thanks again for downloading this book, I hope you enjoy it!

Chapter 1: Preparation for indoor marijuana grow

We are all familiar with the fact that that any way of growing hemp in many countries is completely prohibited, except in special circumstances (if it is sterilized hemp, and psychoactive ingredients were removed; it grows only up to a certain stage). To accomplish this, you need to go through numerous processes, checks and so on.

It is much easier and safer to grow marijuana indoors; it can be it an apartment, a house, a greenhouse, etc. Plants, in this case, grow in the private environment of your home, safe from prying and often very wicked eyes. Similarly, the "home" farming has certain advantages. Plants can be grown throughout a year, and are safe from animals and insects that love to put them on the menu for their lunch (give yourself a bit of imagination, let's imagine a snail eats a few leaves of marijuana during the day).

To be able to grow fine plantlets that will flourish fine, you need to provide them with certain conditions, i.e. at least the minimum in which one will grow fine. The plant requires providing sufficient soil, water and light.

Although it can grow, in a smaller space, it should not be lower than 1.5 meters. Even this height will limit your options, but if you ensure this height, you will be able to grow plantlets fine.

Your room will need an adequate source of ventilation so the air, heat and moisture can circulate freely and change from time to time. The advice is that, if you grow plantlets in the closet, box, you ensure the ventilation by opening the lid or the door at some point during the day. The best location for the plant you will provide if you have a window on the south side of the building. Putting a plant in front of that window, you will ensure the most sunshine. Here you have to be careful that your plant nobody sees, because of restrictions and laws that we are subordinated to (do not give up). If you have a window on the roof of the house, you will solve the problem because your plantlets receive light all day and you will not be in a risk of disclosure.

The most frequent places encountered at home manufacturers are the closet, room or other secluded spots. This way, plants grow under artificial light, and a material that has the capability of reflection will be needed so the plant can get all the possible light that is available. Also, plants require adequate ventilation and air circulation so they can achieve the "working" temperature. With an electric light this problem may occur because they scatter the huge amount of heat, but the following chapter will show how to solve this problem. Also, we need to ensure normal CO2 exchange so the plant can normally perform photosynthesis.

1.1 All you need to start growing weed

1.1.1 The box

The first thing you probably ask yourself is: what kind of box do I actually need? The size of the area for cultivation is determined by the area that the lighting for breeding covers. The height of the space is determined by a plant variety (sativa - high room, cannabis indica - medium, auto-flowering or cannabis ruderalis- lower space). The room must have an opening for the entrance of fresh air (supply air).

It is necessary to monitor the temperature and humidity in the room. Optimal values are: **27 degrees of Celsius in temperature, humidity around 60% during vegetation and 40% during the process of flourishing.**

The interior space must be coated with a material for a better reflection of light:

- Mylar foil - a reflection of 95%

- Black and white foil is 85%

- White matte color - 80%

- Aluminum foil - 75%

Box can be made of PC housings, cabinets, boxes, refrigerators, and there are tents ready for breeding. The possibilities are endless and they only dependent on your imagination.

1.1.2 Basic combat kit

Some basic equipment would be:

Box with associated parts:

If you make a box yourself, pay attention to the power part: buy quality cables, be sure to tighten the connections well. Pay attention to the quality of constructive and effective ventilation.

Soil

Always buy quality soil under the condition that it was stored well in the store. Make it airy and light, make the appropriate mix.

Containers

Properly developed and larger root system will give bigger yield. So do not complain about the size of the containers, until they can fit into the box.

Ph meter

- the most important device which is necessary to have as a part of the equipment. Without it, there is a possibility of inadequate spending of nutrients from the soil, and it can lead to overfeeding and other problems.

Thermo / hygrometer

- the device for measuring temperature and humidity. Always measure the temperature at the top of the plant. Keep the temperature and humidity close to optimal values. The difference in day / night temperature should not be higher than 10 degrees. Low level of humidity attracts insects that prefer dry environment, while the excessive humidity can cause the occurrence of mold in the flowering stage.

Timer

If you do not want to put the lightning on and off every day, get a mechanical (daily) or a digital timer that is capable of managing multiple programs.

Set fertilizers

There is no good yield without food, so get a quality fertilizer for vegetation and flowering, and you can use various auxiliary preparations.

1.1.3 Soil preparations

Purchase quality, sterile soil that contains all that is necessary for the plant growth and development. Selection of some of the better types you will avoid many problems with pests and weeds, and later will start feeding. Some of the better known and better types of soil are: Terra Magma, Compo Sana, Klasmann, Potgrond Terra Brill, etc. Always buy the soil for flowering plants or universal soil. Soil from the garden, as well as those for citrus, orchids, cacti, palm trees…be sure to avoid.

Be aware of the specification of the soil- the PH value should be about 6.5. It is also important for the soil to be airy so the root system is supplied well with the oxygen. Breathability of the soil is gained by adding soil granules like styrofoam or perlite (do not absorb moisture) and vermiculite (moisture absorbing).

It is important to make a good drainage also, and allow the full flow of water from the flower pot. It will be designed by putting a clay beads on the bottom so the water could not retain on the bottom of the container. It is not a bad idea to place them on the soil surface to prevent rapid evaporation of moisture from the soil (less watering).

1.1.4 Air

The area for cultivation must be carried out with good ventilation, which will enable your plant consumption of the fresh air. The air intake is usually performed by a passive inlet vent or with a fan with lesser capacity and is usually placed in the bottom area for the cultivation. For these purposes, PC or bathroom fans can be used.

For the air outlet you need a stronger fan (bathroom fan or turbine) to create a negative pressure due to the faster air exchange in your area, and should be placed at the top of the area where warm air collects.

You also need the oscillating fan that will blow the plants i.e. will imitate the wind and your plants will strengthen, and will mix the air in the box.

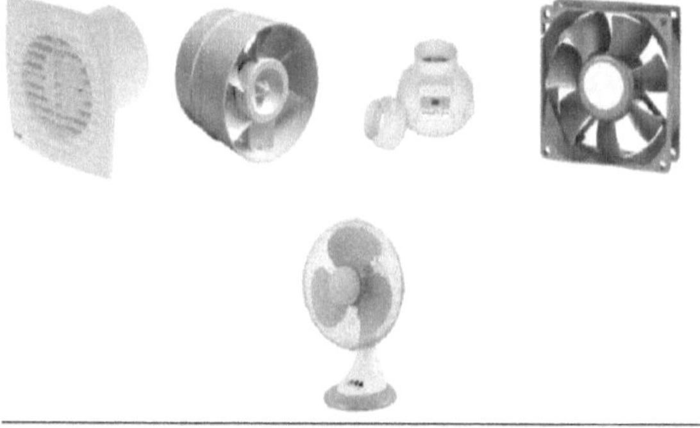

For systems with a strong lighting you should place the so called cool tube, or glass tube in which the light bulb is located. Cool tube is connected to flexible hoses with turbine fan that extracts hot air out of space to grow plats through the filter, which is usually on the other end of the flexible hose.

1.1.5 Lightning

As for the light, the most effective are metal-halide lamp (MH), or the high-pressure-sodium lamps (HPS). These are lamps that are similar to those used for street lighting. MH lamp emits white light, and HPS lights famous orange-violet light that you can see on the lamps for night lighting. HPS lamps emit about one-sixth of light more than MH lamps. Both lamps come with a transformer and cost from about $ 150 to $ 350. Another option is fluorescent lamp. They are made in the form of rods which are interlocked in the basis. With them, there is a problem because they emit light over a large area so it is possible that the light is unnecessarily wasted. Also, they have only half of the power of MH or HPS lamps, meaning they scatter half of the amount of light.

However, fluorescent lamps have certain advantages. They scatter light throughout the tube so that no part of it will be dangerous for the plant, so you can expose plants quite close to this type of lamp. Fluorescent lamps are good because they emit different colors of light. Cold-white (pure white light), warm white (slightly yellow) and daylight correspond to the spectrum, and the types of light. If you can provide one combination of these three spectra, it will be the best combination. If you use this professional lamp, you will need luminance indicative for a good breeding, it is 30W to 50W for HPS and MH lamps. If you use fluorescent tubes, power should be about 40W to 60W. All this refers to one square meter of space. We know that very often it is really expensive to buy these bulbs that cost a lot. Therefore, we are mentioning the alternative when it comes to light. The amount of light is measured in lumens. For the breeding of these beautiful plants we need about 12,000 lumens of light. 8000 lumens would be the optimal amount of light needed for growing. However, plantlets will succeed it with much less light. Suppose it would be good to let it be at least 5,000 lumens.

This amount is equivalent to 5 energy saving lamps. On each bulb should write the amount that is being dispersed during the broadcast, although very often there are bulbs where such data does not exist. Buy those that have the written data.

For healthy plant growth you need 2 types of the spectrum: blue and red. Blue spectrum is used in vegetation stage, and the red in the flowering stage. Although, it is required to add light from other spectrum in each stage (the vegetation stage requires more blue, less red, and the flourishing stage requires more red and less blue spectrum), you will not make mistake if you have completed the entire cultivation with the HPS bulb in red spectrum. Bulbs with blue spectrum are marked 6500 K, and 2200 K with red spectrum.

The best choice for the cultivation of plants is HID bulb: MH - Metal Halide

and HPS - High Pressure Sodium or sodium lamps.

These lamps require a special ballast and ignitor (starter). MH lamps have blue spectrum and are used for vegetation. HPS lamps have red spectrum and are used for flowering.

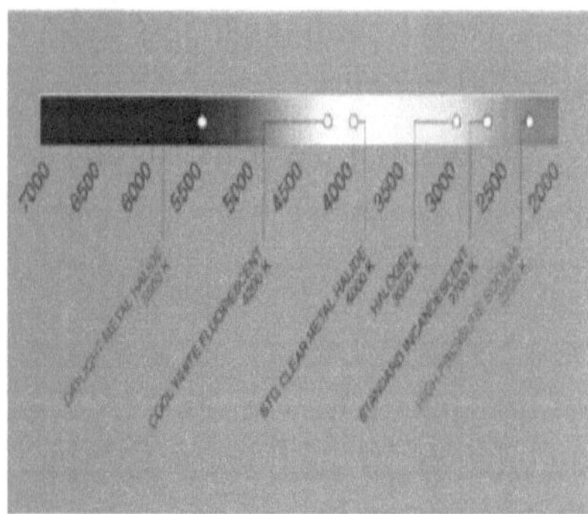

CFL energy saving lamps broadcast less heat than HID lamps, but considering they give less lumen and they are not cheap, their efficiency is questioned. If necessary, use them for smaller spaces. They do not require additional equipment such as ballasts or ignitor.

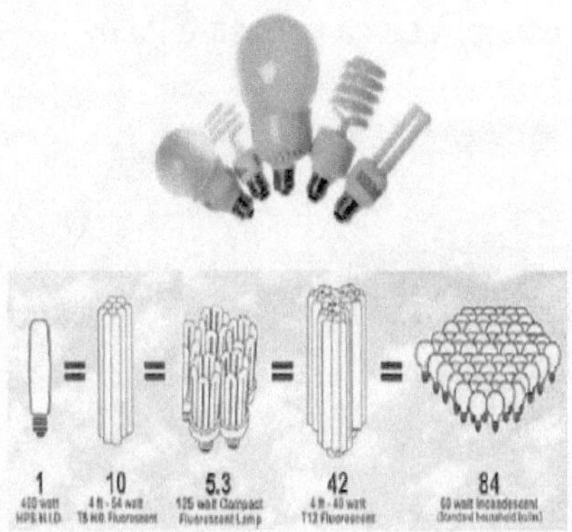

Fluorescent tubes are also less usable considering the lumen, but they are good for the beginning and for vegetation. Bulbs require more power especially the cooling airflow, while the weaker ones can perform without refrigeration. It is necessary to use reflectors so the light would not be wasted in an undesirable direction.

Light is probably one of the most important components of our ritual of growing plants. Spraying the plant will take away her purpose, her personality. Do not spray your plants with anything other than water. Even if you cannot afford top conditions to your plant, the minimum conditions that can be really small would be sufficient to succeed and to grow a large plant. The author's first plantlets is grown in a small closet, with two energy saving lamps, in a jar that was deep twenty cm with diameter of twenty cm. It grew up to 1.3 meters and made beautiful flowers. Love for the plant is the most important part of farming. Without love you cannot get a powerful plant. This is what was forgotten when breeding.

1.1.6 Water

Watering is done when the soil is completely dry. It is time to water the plant when they hang a bit, and show that they are thirsty. You can notice this when the soil separates from the edge of the vessel.

Be sure to measure the PH value of the water. You can measure Ph by testing drops, or use PH meter.

By purchasing something from above (like PH meter), you will avoid a lot of potential problems in breeding. The plant can take nutrients only in a certain range of pH values, so let the check of the pH value be the first thing that you will take care of during farming. If you use the tap water, leave it to rest for a day or two so all the chlorine evaporates from the water. You can lower the Ph value with lemon juice, citric acid, vinegar or some of the finished products to lower the Ph. Sodium bicarbonate and some of the finished products can raise the Ph value.

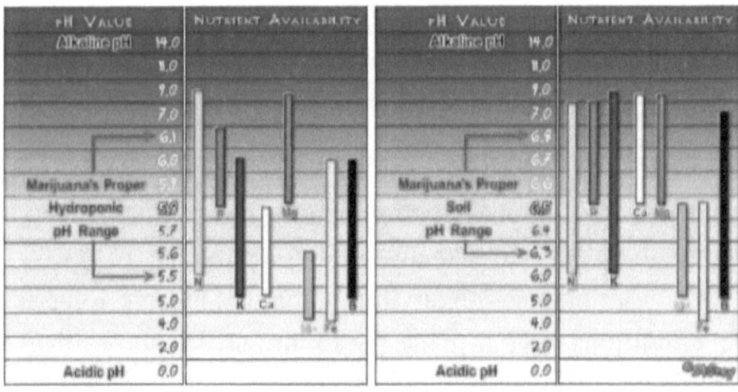

It would not be a bad idea to ventilate the water for watering, and you can do this with air pump i.e. put the air stone into the water and connect it with the silicone hose. Expelling the air through the pump, the water becomes enriched with oxygen.

1.1.7 Preparing the soil and selection of container

First decide how many vessels or pots you want to put in the box. You need at least 40 cm of space for the plant (for example, the box sized 80x80 can grow 4 plants). Do not put too many containers, because there will be too many plants in the box. When you decide which containers you will use, and the number of pieces you will grow, prepare vessels for the soil.

Make holes in the bottom of the bowl, cover the bottom with clay beads. Pour the soil mix you have prepared. Gently press with the palm each layer of the soil, but not too hard. Water it well, and when the soil settles from watering, top up with more soil.

To mix the soil, you can use a combination of several types of soil. Add polystyrene, perlite, vermiculite, sand, etc. You can sort your mix or use some of the recipes for soil mixes found on the Internet.

Chapter 2: Germinating and planting cannabis seeds

There are several solutions: take the seeds from the packets, available from some of the seed banks or make your own seed. When planting the seeds, you do not know the characteristics of plants as well as gender. If you buy the seed in a seed bank, you can choose between regular seeds (a certain percentage of the plants will be male) or feminized seeds (99% female plants). In both cases, characteristics of the variety are known. It is important to note that **you can consume only female plant, male are not welcome** in the pits, because pollination will happen and loss of potency of THC of the pollinated female plants. Male plants are desired only in the target-pollination, in order to obtain seeds.

2.1 Sprouting

You can arrange sprouting seeds this way: place the seeds- put them on a wet handkerchief, coat with another handkerchief and moisten with water. Keep them in a dark, warm place. When the seed sprouts, throw it into the ground and backfill with 2-3 mm of soil.

You can also throw the seeds in a glass of water (adjusted PH), keep them in water for 24-48 hours after they sprout the seed, place them directly into the ground. The seed is planted when the sprout is turned down (this is the root). Cover up containers and day spray the surface of the soil several times a day. Within a few days the plant will come to the surface and the magic begins.

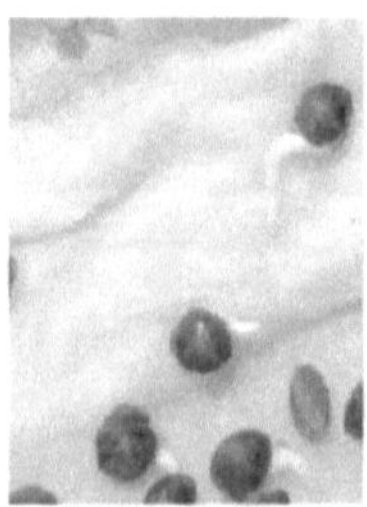

Chapter 3: Vegetation

This phase lasts from the beginning of the growth until the appearance of the first pistil, and it is also called the growing phase. In this phase, are used various modes of lighting: Day / Night - 18/6 hours, 20/4 or even 24/0 hours. More light in the vegetation phase means faster development of branches. In combination with some methods of training, this phase brings rich, branched plant with a lot of foliage.

During vegetation, you should strive to fill the space of the box up to 70%, and also keep the peaks of future flowers at the same level so the light is deployed equally. The simplest method to increase the yield is the -called LST - Low Stress Training (bending branches and stems so the light can come to the non-illuminated peaks and start to grow). When we are satisfied with the size of the plant, we are switching timer on the light mode 12/12 or *the bloom mode*. In practice, the plant is vegetable for about a month, but it all depends on the area and size of pots.

3.1 Blossoming

In nature, flowering begins when day and night last equally, i.e. 12 hours of day and 12 hours of night. By switching the mode timer to 12/12, you encourage the flowering. Few days after switching to the 12/12 mode will appear first pistils (small white hairs that mark the feminine) and it is in fact a real beginning of flowering. Male plants will have little bananas or eggs.

Remove them from the box as soon as possible to prevent pollination. Plant growth and lengthening of the branches will continue in the coming days, the remaining 30% of the space in the box is filled, and the branches and stems are becoming stiffer and harder to bend. After that, growth stops completely, and the flowers are starting to gain weight. Blossoming lasts for 2 months or longer, depending on the variety. If you are causing stress to the plant, flowering can be prolonged. It is important to note that autoflowering or ruderalis species does not depend on the regime of 12/12 mode, and will bloom in any light regime after 20 days.

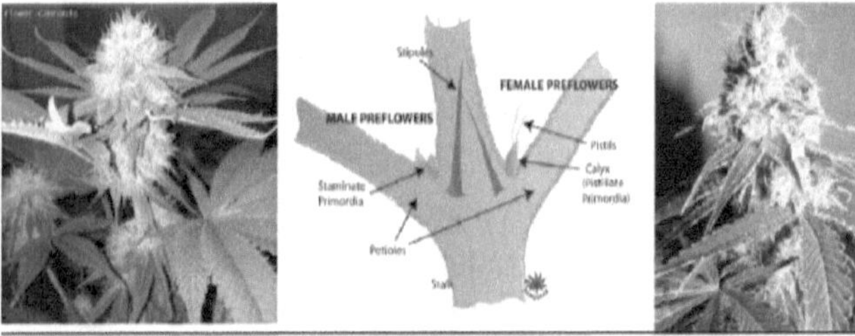

Feeding

If you have purchased a high-quality soil and put containers large enough, there is no need to feed the plant for at least first 2-3 weeks. The time to start feeding it when leaves start yellowing, i.e. it is a sign that the plant spent all the nutrients from the soil and begins to draw them from the leaves. **During growing, you need fertilizer with more nitrogen (N), during flowering you need fertilizer with more phosphorus (P) and potassium (K).** Each fertilizer has specified NPK ratio. Always start to feed with the 1/3 or ½ of the recommended dose, but gradually lift the dose to the recommended.

There is a large selection of fertilizers specially designed for the plant with which it is difficult to go wrong if you stick to the manufacturer's recommendations and tables for fertilization. Recommendation for beginners: Hesi starter package, BioBizz starter pack or Jungle juice.

With a basic fertilizer on the market, there are various additional products that can enhance root development, create more flowers, increase flower's weight gain or simply improve intake of nutrients from the soil.

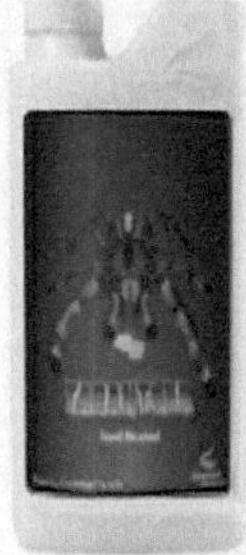

You should perform feeding after watering (or skip one watering session, and feed the next time you're watering the plant), according to the manufacturer's recommended doses, but if you notice signs of overfeeding, skip meals and pour plain water. Proceed with eating with the next watering. It is vital to set the PH value, if is too high or too low, the plant cannot take all the nutrients it needs.

3.2 The washout

About 10 days before the harvest, it is necessary to flush the soil with plenty of water (5 x greater than the volume of the container) so all the fertilizers gathered in the soil are washed well. In the last days the plant will draw nutrients from the last reserves in the leaves and yellow like the autumn is coming. By the end, you should water the plant with pure water, and in the last watering can add a little honey or sugar cane molasses. The last 24-48 hours the plant is left in the dark. According to some theories, secretion of

THC is then increased, but more likely this is because of the decomposition of chlorophyll, and because of the better taste when drinking. The washout is also desirable during overfeeding, and it is desirable to practice it during cultivation to flush toxic salts that accumulate on the roots.

Chapter 4: The harvest

What time is the best time to harvest the plant, will tell us the view of the microscope on the trichomes, whose range can go from colorless to milk-in-color and red colored. Prematurely harvested plant will have colorless trichomes, which means it has not reached sufficient maturity. When all the trichomes are red, it is about time for the harvest, because the delay will cause further declines of THC. "Milky" trichomes cause "head high" and red cause "body high". Harvest when trichomes are half milk / half red and you will get a bit of both.

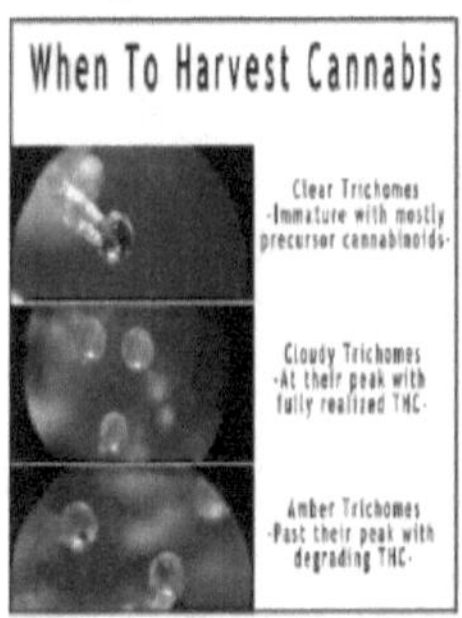

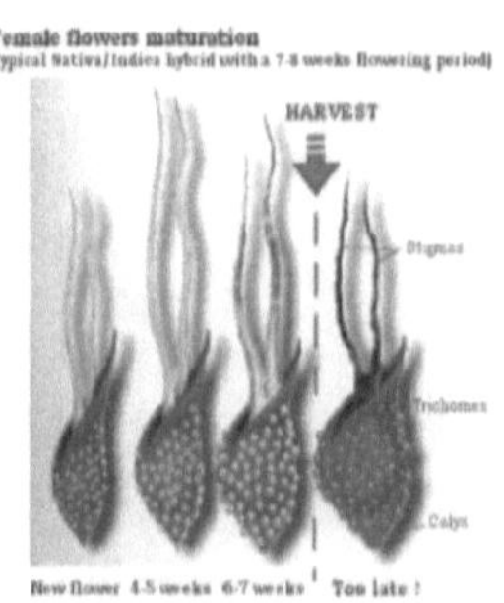

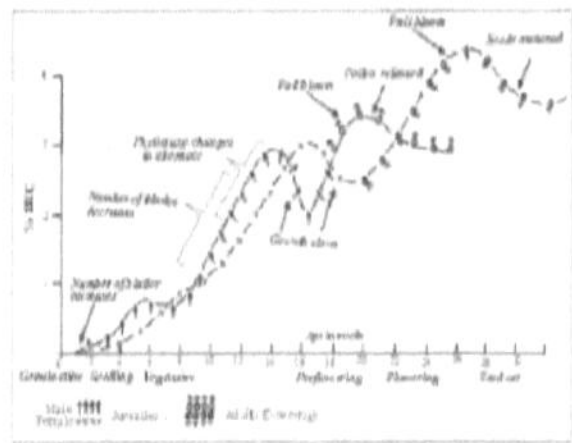

4.1 Drying

When you cut down all the peaks along with the part of the stem, it is time to cut off all the leaves, and "haircut" those close to the peaks.

Make series from flower peaks on the rope and hang upside down in a dark place (chlorophyll disintegrates in the dark) with good air circulation. Make sure that tops of the flowers do not touch each other. If dried in a ventilated box, make sure that tops are not directly imposed to the fan.

After a few days of drying (depending on the room temperature and humidity) peaks are dry. You will recognize dried peaks by the fact that the stem can break easily. After that, put peaks in jars and seal them with the lid. Open the jar every day, stir peaks and allow the change of the air in the jar.

The process of "taking care" can last from several weeks to several months. Be patient, and flowers will be tastier and "more potent".

4.2 Breeding techniques

LST - Low Stress Training

This is the technique of bending the branches with the help of the ropes, wires, etc. so the parts of the plant that normally stand in the shade are illuminated and encouraged to grow. Gently bend the branches not to break them. While the plant is young, warping is easier to perform, and when the plant is older branches and stems become stronger and stiffer and harder to bend and easy to rupture. By warping the branches try to bring all the peaks at the same level of brightness for more balanced deployment of light.

High Stress Training - Topping, Super Cropping

Topping is performed so that the main peak is cut off from the plant, after which protrude two new peaks. Topping can be done several times, and it should be performed only during the vegetation phase. Secondary peaks can be topped also. After topping, plant relives stress and temporarily the growth stops. After topping, leave the plant for some time to be able to develop tops.

Topped Plant After 2 Days

FIM

This method implies to remove the part of the peak after which will grow four new. After the treatment, the plant goes through stress and the growth stops for a while.

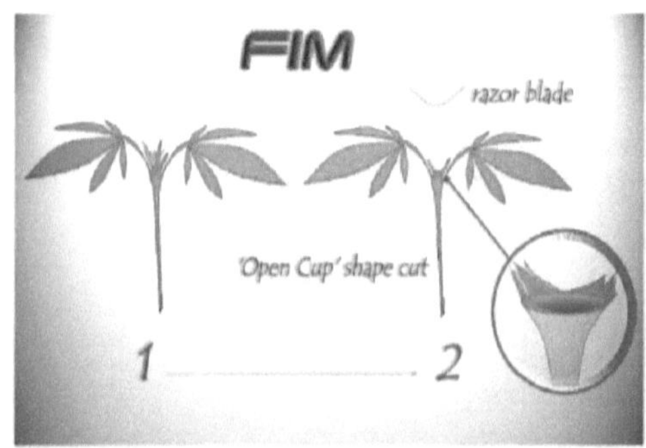

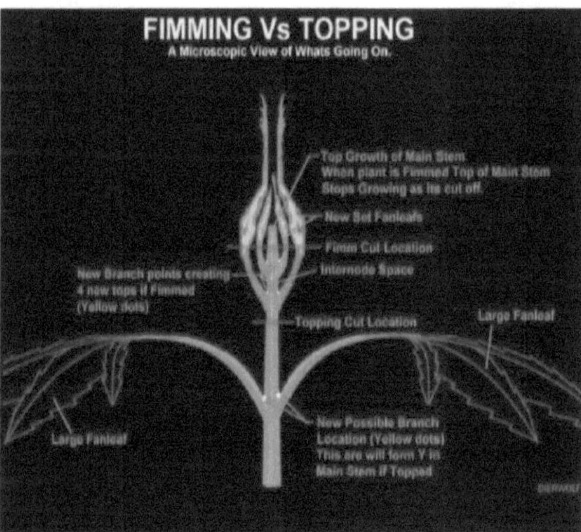

Super Cropping

If the tops grow too high, and the higher branches cannot bent, use a technique Super Cropping. Break the branch- let it be half broken. After a few days, on a broken place will grow a node, the broken place will heal and the top will continue to grow toward the light.

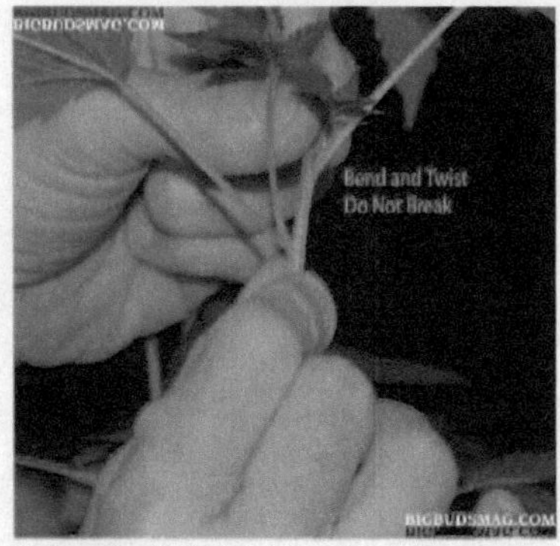

Chapter 5: The most common mistakes to avoid when growing marijuana

5.1 Eating disorders

If you pour the water that has no adjusted pH value, it is possible to disrupt the proper intake of nutrients from the soil, therefore nourish it regularly with the set PH value, adhering to the prescribed dose of fertilizer manufacturers.

5.2 Parasites

Sometimes, in your box will come unwanted tenants (red spider, fruit flies -
fungus gnats, symphilids, thrips, leaf miners, etc.) that will attack your plant
from above and below (the root). To prevent them, use of the sterile soil, hold
moisture close to the optimum value, not putting the plant out of the box (for
example, to the terrace, and the like), because there is a great possibility that
you will enter a pest in the box. There are also preventive agents such as
Neem, a natural pesticide, which effectively protects plants from
microorganisms and parasites. It can be added to the mix of soil, watered or
sprayed. You can use hydrogen peroxide or put the ladybug in the box, which
is a natural predator. All the problems with pests solve instantly in order not
to spread and destroy all your hard work.

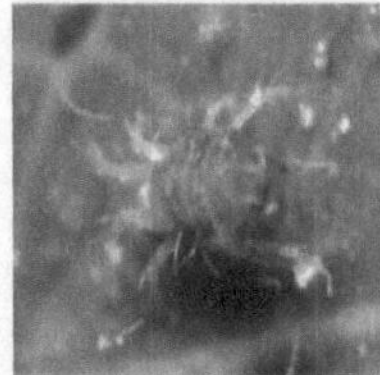  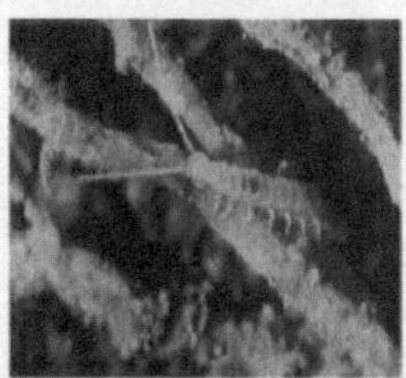

Red spider (Spider mites) - the most dangerous of all the problems, it is
very difficult to solve. It is sucking juices from the leaves, leaving white
spots where they feed. Neem is effective against spiders, increasing the
moisture and tobacco extract.

Fruit flies (Fungus gnats) - Adult flies lay their eggs on the surface of the
soil from which collect larvae. The larvae feed with roots and organic matter.
This problem can be solved when on the surface of the soil you put slices of
potato that collect larvae. After they are gathered, discard potatoes. You can
also cover the surface of the soil with sand, it will suffocate larvae. Neem and
the tobacco extract are also effective.

Symphilid - white or light colored and look like caterpillars. They dig the
ground and feed with roots. When watering, it is easy to observe them as they
rise to the surface. The effective means against them are Neem and hydrogen
peroxide.

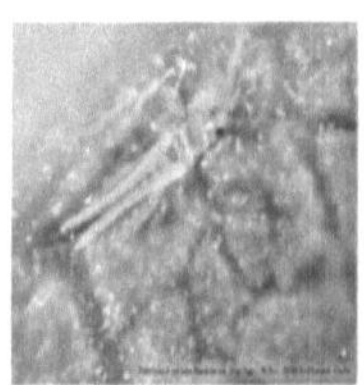  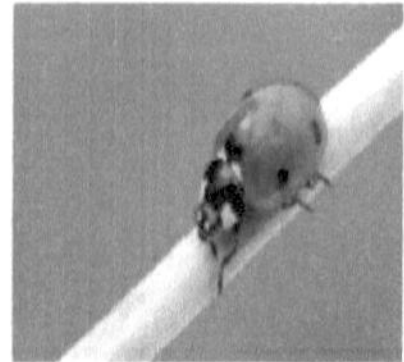

Thrips - very small but can be seen with the naked eye. They reproduce quickly, and some species are more resistant to chemicals. They suck the juice from the leaves, and the leaves may appear white. They're attracted to the yellow color, but garlic rejects them. Neem and ladybug are their natural enemy.

Leaf miners - they eat leaves and dig trenches to lay their larvae. You will recognize them by carved lines on the leaves. Against these pests Neem is an effective agent.

5.3 Problems with feeding

Heat stress: Look at the picture below and you will see brownish edges on the leaves that indicate heat damage stress. This indicates problems with feeding, but these are leaves from the top of the plant. They were closest to the lamps and heat damaged them. The only solution is to increase the distance between plants and lamps.

The problem with feeding:

The symptoms that are seen in the picture bellow in most cases indicate that manure i.e. food was sprayed on the leaves of a plant that was under hot lamps, causing "roasting" of the leaves.

Figure 3 shows the very beginning of the process of "roasting" caused by food, and it is common in hydroponic farming systems. It can be assumed that the plant has all the necessary nutrients that it can use, and everything else is redundant. The redundant food affects badly on the plant. Feed the plant less frequently and reduce the food dose for a short period of time.

Figure 4 clearly shows that it comes to overfeeding. High level of nutrients accumulates in the leaves which caused drying and damage as seen on the picture. You have to "rinse" the plant, and water it abundantly with clean water (preferably distilled) to help the roots to recover and to prevent further damaging. The next thing to do is to find the cause of such high levels of nutrients and to correct it.

Excessive watering:

Plants in Figure 5 were on constant watering system, which aims to make the entire root system continuously receive water and food. Better solution would be to feed the plants, say for like 30 minutes, every 2-3 hours. This schedule would allow oversaturated root to "rest" and to reach for air it needs, and this would reduce the possibility of destroying the root and the emergence of other problems.

The photo shows an attempt to rescue the plant.

Unstable pH: Both leaves on Figures 6 and 7 are from the same plant. Some would think that this is because of the excessive food but this is much more like a drastic decline in pH value. Too high or too low pH can block nutrients in the form of salts and compounds and some of them can be toxic for the plant. The next mistake mainly happens when the manufacturer tries to boost consumption, which is making it worse. PH value drops even more and blocks further consumption of nutritious. You should stop the feeding, measure the pH value and return it to its normal.

Ozone damages:

This is rare but not non-existent problem. It has been noticed that this usually occurs in the vicinity of the generator, and the main problem is a lack of magnesium.

"Moving" elements:

Lack of the "moving" elements you'll probably notice first on the older leaves, and in the case of the need for these elements the problem will spread on new, young parts of the plant.

Nitrogen (N)

Nitrate-ammonium can be found in organic and inorganic form in the plant, and it combines with carbon, hydrogen, oxygen and sulfur sometimes, to create amino acids, amino enzymes, nucleic acids, chlorophyll and alkaloids. Nitrogen is comparatively high in relation to the molecular weight of proteins in the tissues of the plant.

The plants need a lot of nitrogen during the vegetative phase, but the plant can easily "overdose". If you overdo the plant with nitrogen, pour a large amount of water. Too much nitrogen delays flowering process. It is desirable to cause a shortage of nitrogen before the end of flowering, in order to enrich the taste.

The lack of nitrogen:

Plants will show a lack of power, the growth process will slow down and the plant will act weak. The quality and yield will be significantly lowered. The older leaves will become yellow due to lack of chlorophyll, and perhaps they will fell off the plant. The twigs and the lower parts of the plant will get a purple color.

As you can see on the picture bellow, the increased spending of nitrogen is quite normal in the final stages of flowering.

Poisoning with nitrogen: can be noticed on leaves; they often become dark green. In the case when you seriously overdone with nitrogen, leaves will start to dry and fell off the pant. The root system will remain under-developed, or will be useless over time. Flowers will be deformed and there will be less than usual. The resistance on the stress will be dramatically decreased.

Phosphorus (P) Phosphorus is a component made of certain enzymes and proteins, triphosphate (ATP), ribonucleic acids (RNA) and deoxyribonucleic acid (DNA). ATP is involved in various reactions of an energy transfer, and the RNA and DNA are components of the genetic information.

Lack of phosphorus: On figure 11 you can see a serious lack of phosphorus during the phase of flowering. Leaves around the flowers are dark green and red (or purple) and they can become yellow. Rest of the leaves can bend, curl, get a brownish color and fell off. Lack of phosphorus is shown in slow growth, weak plants with dark green or purple pigmentation in older leaves and branches.

Certain phosphorus deficiency during flowering is normal, but excessive defect must be rectified.

Certain care should be taken when determining problems because in some species it is genetically determined to get a purple pigment, but also, this can be a symptom of some other accompanying problems. Thus, be careful and patient.

The figure bellow shows the lack of phosphorus during the vegetative growth. People often make mistake thinking it is a fungal disease. But if you take a closer look you can see that this occurs near the edges of the leaves, and leaves become dark gray with very brittle compounds.

Phosphorus poisoning: extremely rare, and may be associated with the availability and stability of copper and zinc.

Potassium (K)

Potassium is essential in maintaining a "level" of water in the plant, it is also necessary for the accumulation and transfer of carbohydrates. The lack of potassium will reduce the quality and quantity of yield.

Potassium deficiency: Older leaves will look like the problem has just begun, but soon dark "wounds", i.e. dead tissue will appear on them. Symptoms first appear on the top and the edge of the leaves. Branches can become weak and brittle, and the plant may seem obviously thinner. It will be clear that the plant is sick or poisoned. It may look as if it was a lack of iron since the peaks of the plant look "curly" and the edges would "burn up" and die.

Too much sodium (Na) will cause a shortage of potassium. The sources of high salinity, which leads to a lack of potassium, are: sodium bicarbonate (which usually serves to raise the pH, "pH-up"), too much fertilizer, and usage of filters for "water softening". If you have the problem with sodium, pour large amounts of clean water and determine what is the cause of the problem, and try to solve it. Potassium may be reduced because of too much calcium (Ca), or nitrogen, and possibly because of the cold water.

Potassium poisoning: It is rare, but if there is too high a level of potassium, it can decrease the absorption of magnesium, manganese, zinc and iron, and can also affect the availability of calcium.